PERFECTING
THE PASTOR'S ART

D0963796

PERFECTING THE PASTOR'S ART

WISDOM

from AVERY LEE AND GARDNER TAYLOR

G. AVERY LEE AND GARDNER C. TAYLOR

JUDSON PRESS

PUBLISHERS SINCE 1824

VALLEY FORGE, PA

PERFECTING THE PASTOR'S ART
Wisdom from Avery Lee and Gardner Taylor

© 2005 by Judson Press
Valley Forge, PA 19482-0851
All rights reserved.

No part of this publication may be reproduced, stored in a retrieval system, or transmitted in any form or by any means, electronic, mechanical, photocopying, recording, or otherwise, without the prior permission of the copyright owner, except for brief quotations included in a review of the book.

Unless otherwise noted, Bible quotations in this volume are from the New Revised Standard Version of the Bible, copyright © 1989 by the Division of Christian Education of the National Council of the Churches of Christ in the United States of America. Used by permission. All rights reserved. Bible quotations marked **KJV** are from the King James Version of the Bible.

Library of Congress Cataloging-in-Publication Data
Lee, G. Avery.
Perfecting the pastor's art : wisdom from Avery Lee and Gardner Taylor / G. Avery Lee and Gardner C. Taylor.
    p. cm.
ISBN 0-8170-1482-9 (alk. paper)
1. Pastoral theology. I. Taylor, Gardner C. II. Title.
BV4011.3.L44 2005
253—dc22

2005002480

Printed in the U.S.A.

13 12 11 10 09 08 07 06 05

10 9 8 7 6 5 4 3 2 1

To Gladys Lee (deceased wife)
—G. Avery Lee

To all who find in Christ fellowship
with all others who find the same blessing
Avery and I found across many years.
—Gardner C. Taylor

CONTENTS

AVERY LEE AND GARDNER TAYLOR have been friends—good friends—since the 1940s. Dr. Lee recalls, "I was associate pastor at First Baptist Church of Baton Rouge. Lots of people were talking about this great young preacher in town, and I knew they weren't talking about me. I found out that his name was Gardner Taylor. He was pastor at First Mt. Zion Baptist Church, known then as a Negro congregation. I went over to meet him. I'll never forget that his office at the time was under a stairwell."

Dr. Taylor continues the story. "Avery came to my office. We talked a bit and became friends. It blossomed from there. Avery's wife, Ann, and my wife, Laura, became good friends as well. The four of us would get together at our homes. We had a wonderful fellowship."

In the 1940s, for black persons and white persons to get together socially was somewhat radical. Pastor Lee recalls, "We raised some eyebrows. I'm sure there were some people in both of our congregations who were a bit upset."

Pastor Taylor has a slightly different recollection. "It wasn't *some* of them. It was *most* of them. In those days, the patterns of segregation were so sharp, so severe, so frozen that it was more than unusual for a white person and a black person to develop the kind of friendship that Avery and I had."

Rev. Taylor left Baton Rouge in 1948 for Concord Baptist Church in Brooklyn, New York, but he says, "Our friendship did not suffer because of the distance." The two men, now in their late 80s, stayed in touch regularly through the years, getting together whenever the opportunity arose. In 1998, St. Charles Avenue Baptist Church in New Orleans, which Avery Lee served from 1961 to 1980, inaugurated the Avery and Glad Lee Preaching Series in honor of its former pastor and his wife. The inaugural preacher was an old friend of Avery's, Gardner C. Taylor. Others have included Martin Marty and Barbara Brown Taylor.

In this book Drs. Lee and Taylor share for the benefit of others, particularly those just starting out in pastoral ministry, some of what they have learned during over a century's worth of combined experience in pastoral ministry. They address a variety of topics, ranging from sermon preparation and preaching to church administration to dealing with difficult people. They share not only their successes, but also, at times, their failures and insecurities, for there is something to be learned from these as well.

Many will be surprised to discover that Dr. Taylor, best known for his exemplary work in the pulpit, actually dreaded that long walk to the sanctuary each week before the Sunday service. Readers will learn about how this famed preacher put together his sermons week after week.

Meanwhile, Dr. Lee's unusual wit and unbridled sense of humor shine through in this candid resource. So does his prophetic voice, his commitment to speak his mind, even if it meant there would be some people who, in his words, "wanted to run me out of town."

One of Avery Lee's favorite sayings is a German proverb: "We grow too soon old, too late smart." Fortunately, however, both Avery Lee and Gardner Taylor got smart long before they got old. And in this resource they share some of their wisdom, wisdom that deserves to be recognized, even cherished, by both current and future generations.

THE CALL TO MINISTRY

THE NATURE OF THE CALL

Gardner Taylor: In the book of Revelation there are twelve gates to the heavenly city, not one. In similar fashion, when it comes to how God calls persons to ministry, I believe that there is no one pattern, no single prescription. God deals with us individually, because each person is unique. Each person responds to God's call in accordance with his or her personality.

But although there is no single pattern, one could say that there are common elements. One such element is a sense of pressure, a feeling that something is not as it ought to be, a feeling of dissatisfaction or, as a friend of mine used to call it, "dis-ease" about what one is doing. It's a pull, a compulsion, an urging, an agitation, something that is not precisely defined or easily described.

I believe that God, not only in his creativity, but also out of his respect for us, does not bring things down to a blueprint. It's more a prospectus, an outline, a suggestion of what ought to be. This being the case, there may be an element of doubt or uncertainty that is never fully removed. Certainly at the outset of a call, this element of doubt is important. Those who feel called but have doubts are able to identify with the people to whom they are ministering, who also will have doubts. Someone in ministry who talks about being without doubt might be viewed as an alien from another planet. Doubt belongs to existence. One could even argue that to have true validity, the pastor's call *must* include an element of doubt.

The sense of pressure or discomfort that accompanies a call is something that can be denied or avoided at one's discretion. One may say no to it. Response to a call will be determined largely by the person who is being called. Some of us respond more easily and more quickly and more obediently. Others of us are more stubborn, more reluctant, more hesitant for many different reasons. We have to recognize this variation in personality. Phillips Brooks, for instance, tried to teach, but he couldn't get away from the feeling that pastoral ministry was his calling. On the other hand, Charles Spurgeon's response was immediate. He went to a church on Artillery Street in London on a stormy day, heard a preacher, and at age seventeen knew that this was what he was supposed to do.

Avery Lee: Being called by God is clearly a valid biblical concept. In the Bible both men and women were called by God to do something specific. Sometimes that became a lifetime of service to God. At other times it might have been a one-time deed. Moses' call, for example, was both. The call of Joshua and Caleb was a specific call that developed into a larger arena. Deborah was called to be a judge in Israel, while

Esther's call was more of a declaration of who she was and an identification of herself with both God and her people. The New Testament speaks of Jesus calling the twelve apostles, Saul of Tarsus, and others. The "call of God" is for different ministries to different people. That's the case in the Bible, and it's the case for us today.

We must remember that for all persons, the first call is to accept Jesus Christ as our Savior and then follow him in our daily lives. When it comes to a specific call to ministry, it's not the same for everyone. For some, the call comes early in life, as it did for me. For others, it comes later, and it may involve a career change. I know of a young man who grew up in our church, received his law degree, and was practicing law in Houston, Texas. He was married and had children. The mysterious call of God came to him. He listened and gave an affirmative answer. He went on to seminary and then to an internship with a Methodist church.

Gardner Taylor: I wanted to go into law with an emphasis on criminal law. I did not want to be a preacher. In fact, years after I began in ministry, I still had questions, doubts. I wasn't sure. Frankly, I wasn't sure that this was something a fairly healthy-minded young person ought to be doing. I say this in part to encourage young men and women in ministry who have doubts of their own. A passage in the book of Habakkuk says that if the vision tarries, wait—it will surely come. And I think that the intervening period in which someone has very serious questions about whether he or she is truly called is a part of the doubt process and is crucial to successful ministry.

Doubts ought not prevent those who feel this sense of calling from moving forward with outstretched arms. The plateau likely will change. In ministry there will be desert stretches during which one feels sure about almost nothing. There will be times when one's faith wears very thin and he or she may not feel anything but frustration. These times have to be endured. This is part of Paul's counsel to Timothy: endure hardship as a good soldier. A person who is going to minister to people must speak to their doubt but also must speak to this need to endure.

Avery Lee: I was converted to Christ as a teenager at a Pentecostal rally. I didn't remain a Pentecostal for long. I joined the Exchange Avenue Baptist Church in Oklahoma City. That church had an annual "Decision Service" for high school students in which the call of God for preachers or missionaries was presented, and the young people were asked to make a decision. Some quiet inner voice seemed to be saying to me that my call in life was to declare God's good news. There was no emotional upheaval, no resistance to some superior force like Saul experienced on the road to Damascus. Instead, it seemed to be the natural thing for me to do. It was a voluntary enlistment for the duration, a commitment of life to preaching and pastoral ministry. From that day to this one, there has never been any question that this was the right decision for me.

There have been doubts and struggles across seven decades of ministry—fighting and fears within and without. I have questioned the branches but never the Tree. Many branches have been cut away, but the Tree still stands.

Others' experiences will be different. Some question the call, perhaps fight against it until they give in. The call of God ultimately is a mystery, but I think I can safely say that there is no single formula.

Gardner Taylor: A call to ministry can be influenced by life events and by how we interpret them. My call came about partly as a result of a horrible car accident in the spring of 1937. I was nineteen at the time and a chauffeur for James A. Bacoats, the president of my little college. We were on a rural road in a 1934 Dodge sedan thirteen miles from Baton Rouge when a Model T Ford cut across in front of us. I hit it head-on, and it bounced off the highway. The two men in the car that we hit, both of them white, were killed. The only two witnesses were two white men, one of whom was a local Southern Baptist preacher, Jesse Sharkey. This was a time when, no matter the details or specifics, no black person could ever be in the right. But these two men went to the inquest the next morning at the parish courthouse and told exactly what had happened. The officials accepted their testimony. I was in too much of a state of shock to realize right away the deliverance I had received. But I definitely felt the prayers of others for me. A few days later, I walked into the president's office and told him that I wanted to be a preacher.

There is irony in this story, because I'd had a distaste for the ministry. My father was a pastor, and I greatly admired him. But I'd read a book by Robert Ingersoll, *Some Mistakes of Moses*, in which the author had raised doubts about certain events in the Scriptures. Now, some of the fellows at my college, including H. Beecher Hicks Sr., had already declared themselves for ministry. I'd had a lot of fun pointing out these discrepancies in the Scriptures to these young men in the dormitory. Today I feel almost a sense of shame for it, but at the time I enjoyed it. Well, needless to say, I took it on the chin in the dormitory when President Bacoats announced in chapel that I wanted to enter the ministry.

HELPING OTHERS RECOGNIZE A CALL

Gardner Taylor: Pastors first ought to counsel others to maintain an openness to God. In fact, this applies not just when it comes to a call to ministry. In every instance, openness on our part is required in order for God to deal with us. God does not overpower people. So we move forward by hint, by suggestion, by feeling, by reading, by studying, by reflection. The

Bible tells us that God stands at the door and knocks. Human beings have the capacity to say no, even to God. Perhaps the time is not right.

I'm very leery of pastors who say, "You need to do this, you need to do that." But pastors are in a position to set down guidelines that can be applied to people's lives and vocations. These should be understood as indicatives, not imperatives.

Avery Lee: I've talked with young people through the years about the possibility of them making ministry their life's vocation. Although the call of God comes with an element of mystery, I feel that it's legitimate to look for indicators. Take, for example, someone who is particularly involved with the youth group and shows a deep interest in the things of the faith. Or maybe someone has good people skills and speaks well in public. Pastors should not be shy about urging young people to be open to God's call. Then, if and when that person is called, he or she will be ready.

THE PASTOR'S ROLE AND WORK

FOUNDATIONS OF PASTORAL MINISTRY

Avery Lee: Karl Barth was arguably the twentieth century's greatest theologian. The story goes that one time he was lecturing somewhere, and during the question-and-answer period, he was asked to summarize his theology. After a brief pause, he responded, "Jesus loves me, this I know, for the Bible tells me so." This is what it all boils down to: Jesus' love is for each of us as individuals. The pastor needs to believe this more than anything else. A person who feels loved by God, is loved at home, and has a sense of worth and purpose can take anything that life or pastoral ministry throws his or her way.

AN AWESOME TASK

Avery Lee: I once heard a Roman Catholic priest speak to a group of Protestant clergy. He said, in effect, "We are not only representatives of the presence of God, but also representatives of the absence of God." To be viewed by others as representatives of God is a daunting responsibility, especially in light of the possibility that others will see not God's presence, but God's absence. Recognizing this ought to inspire the pastor to take his or her work very seriously. Some will see in us a blurred image. We should do our best to make the image clearer. And we should remind others that although some may see pastors as being in some way unique, the responsibility to represent the presence of God and not the absence rests upon all Christians.

CHARACTERISTICS OF THE PASTOR

Gardner Taylor: A pastor must have not just an interest in Scripture, but a hunger for it. In my earliest years I was influenced toward the ministry (although I didn't realize it) by my mother sitting on our front porch on South Boulevard in Baton Rouge and reading to me *Great Stories of the Bible Illustrated for Children.* It was a purple-back book. I was profoundly touched by the story of Moses in that little crib, and by the story of David taking on Goliath.

The pastor also ought to have some sense of the heartbreak of God—almost a feeling of sympathy for God, who offers himself to us in love—and a desire to make God known to people. Pastors should possess an almost innate restlessness in their search for something real in their lives. Perhaps they read biographies out of an interest to see how other people have lived for good or for ill.

And I do not see how anybody could be in pastoral ministry without a love for people, although that's the hardest thing to come by. I had a friend in Brooklyn, Rabbi Eugene Sack, who used to say that the kingdom of God would be a wonderful thing if people were not in it. And I recall another Mother Teresa, who centuries ago lived in the cloisters for four decades and who said that after having lived with the saints for over forty years, she understood why Jesus chose to live with the sinners. People can be very hard to love.

But beyond all this skepticism and cynicism regarding human nature, there must be an understanding of the struggles that people go through, including the struggle to come to some understanding of what life is all about. And I don't think that a life can be understood apart from the revelation of Scripture. I know I've had people in my own family who were not Christians. They were wonderful people, but I always had the feeling that something was lacking in their lives. So part of the longing of the pastor is to bring others within God's fold.

A PERSONAL PRESCRIPTION

Avery Lee: One of the most expressive statements about the task of a pastor and the church came from the late D. T. Niles of Ceylon (now Sri Lanka). When he was general secretary of the World Council of Churches, he described the proclamation of the gospel as being "one beggar telling another beggar where he found bread." This is who and what we are as pastors: we are essentially passers of the Bread of Life to the hungry, one by one.

Take a close look at the ways that Jesus passed the bread of life, how he dealt with people when they asked him how they could enter this "kingdom" and have the "eternal life" that he was talking about. To Nicodemus he said, "Be born again and start all over" (John 3:7). To a lawyer, "Be a good neighbor" (Luke 10:36–37). To a rich young man, "Get rid of your possessions" (Matthew 19:21). To a crippled man, "Get up and walk" (John 5:8). To a blind man, "Go and wash in the pool" (John 9:7).

There is no single patent medicine for life in the parish ministry. There are only personal prescriptions. Find them and use them. In doing so, we follow Jesus' model.

A PHILOSOPHY OF PRAGMATISM

Avery Lee: College courses in philosophy introduce concepts such as idealism, realism, and pragmatism. I developed a ministerial philosophy of pragmatism, recognizing and operating with the tension between the *Is* (realism) and the *Ought* (idealism). The mission of the pastor can be described as the effort to bring the *Is* and the *Ought* together, even while knowing that we will never fully succeed.

THE IMPORTANCE OF PREACHING

Gardner Taylor: In the black church it is important for the pastor to have the ability to preach. Black congregations are composed of people who are marginalized in this society, people who struggle, sometimes subconsciously, with their sense of significance, of counting. This is both a problem and an opportunity for the pastor, but the opportunity cannot be seized apart from a person's true love for people. A pastor who loves the people can move beyond their stubbornness and eccentricities. Preachers must recognize that they too can be stubborn and eccentric. Such recognition can deliver them from a lot of anxiety, anger, and disdain. It's essential for these kinds of sensitivities to come through in the pastor's preaching.

ENGAGING THE WORLD

Avery Lee: In order to be effective in reaching the community and the world, it's important for the pastor not to be cloistered. Go to the places where people are talking about things that are important to them. Back in my day, it was the local barbershop. I realize that times have changed, but pastors would do well to join a civic club such as Rotary, Kiwanis, or Lions. There you rub shoulders with the movers and shakers of the town or city. Mine was the Kiwanis Club. These clubs do many fine things, and a pastor can be a part of what they do.

A pastor who wants to be regarded as a "real person" has to spend time with "real people." I played golf, and thus I established friendships with both saints and sinners. I heard a lot of words on the golf course that I didn't hear at church—especially when someone missed a three-foot putt or sliced a drive. But being there and making friends were important parts of my ministry. Many of these people, despite their rough edges, were a lot more fun to be around than some Christians, who of all people have most reason to be joyful and cheerful.

Some of the men with whom I played golf were educated, witty, congenial, and good conversationalists. They often referred to themselves as atheists, which I don't believe they were. I looked at this as an opportunity to engage and instruct these men. I even baptized a few of them.

I also tried to be creative when it came to outreach ministries. I think that the most fascinating was an off-beat ministry that I called "Chaplain of a Soda Fountain Congregation." We met in a drugstore across the street from the church, a place that might be compared to a Starbucks today. It was the mid-'60s, the heyday of the "flower children" and "hippies." The group included social dropouts, but also retirees, who represented the establishment. Oddly enough, there was rapport among them. They accepted each other as they were, even if they didn't accept each other's viewpoints.'

Among the dropouts were merit scholars, one with a master's degree in drama, an artist, one called "Crazy Horse" (whose real name we never learned), and a female model who posed in lingerie and sometimes in the nude. The retirees included a stockbroker, an amateur archaeologist, a junior high school teacher, and a freelance entrepreneur.

The group included Protestant, Catholic, Jew, and agnostic. The younger ones gathered because it was economical, while the retirees enjoyed coming to wait for the final edition of the daily newspaper.

At first, I was an outsider. They were suspicious of anyone who represented the church—dropouts because I represented the "establishment," retirees because I, as a Baptist, might try to proselytize them. I'd ask to join them. They were polite but distant. I'd listen, join in the conversation, and leave religion out of the talk. Gradually, I gained their confidence and was accepted.

As for religion, the dropouts were into mystical Eastern religions and meditation. The retirees maintained whatever they had grown up doing. Finally, I was allowed to discuss the Christian faith with them. They were enamored with the Baptist principle of "soul freedom," but they couldn't understand how Baptists could be literal dogmatists within that freedom. Neither could I.

I wish I could say that my persuasiveness made some converts. That didn't happen, but still, ministry took place. The artist and the model were living together "without benefit of clergy." At the sixth month of pregnancy, they decided to get married, and they asked me to do the ceremony. The groom's parents were to celebrate their twenty-fifth wedding anniversary. He asked me to be present for them to repeat their marriage vows. His parents were reconciled to the church, although he, despite my hopes, was not.

The Jewish entrepreneur was a lonely bachelor. His brother, a prominent attorney, died. I was the "unofficial rabbi" who helped him in his grief and got him back on good terms with his own rabbi and synagogue. He later did volunteer work with the Jewish community center.

Many of these "extended church" members would come to church to hear our excellent music, from Bach to Webern, or to see our annual Membership Arts Festival. The artist contributed some of his paintings and even sold a few. Seldom would they come to hear a sermon, but they would come by my office to talk on a personal level about themselves and their dreams.

As that turbulent period limped to a halt, the youth began to rejoin the world. They would come by and tell me that they were going back to graduate school or getting a job. And later they'd come in to give a progress report. The grapevine got word that Robin, the amateur archaeologist, was in Charity Hospital. He had no known family. They asked me to look after him. I did—we all did—until he died.

The drugstore took out the soda fountain, and the old-timers had no place to meet. I offered them the church. They declined but came by from time to time to chat and report on themselves.

Was I a failure for lack of conversions? I think not. Reminders of their heritage and the seeds of Christian faith were planted. I was responsible for the planting. The harvest, Paul reminds us, depends on God: "I planted, Apollos watered, but God gave the growth" (1 Corinthians 3:6). I miss that congregation. They enriched me.

"WHAT I DIDN'T LIKE ABOUT MINISTRY"

Gardner Taylor: One of the things that I did not look forward to was visitation. And I felt condemned for feeling this way. Sick visits always wore very heavily on me, and I'm afraid that I frequently didn't do what I might have done, although I did make the effort. My father said something that I didn't understand as a child. He said that he could hardly bear seeing people with whom he had worked sick and struggling. I certainly understood it when I got older. I didn't relish seeing them either.

In my congregation there were always forty or fifty people on the sick list. I couldn't see all of them, so first there was the question of deciding which of them I was going to try to see. And the next hurdle was getting up and going there to do it. I could find a thousand things to do in the office to delay my visiting. Ironically, once I went, I would find these visits to be among the most rewarding parts of my ministry. I was frequently inspired by the gallantry and courage of people under extreme difficulty. I would get a great deal of preaching material out of those sick visits. Even so, I did not handle this well.

Avery Lee: As I suspect is the case with many pastors, I never liked overseeing the administrative details, especially when the offering didn't meet budget and we had to decide what to reduce. I felt neither qualified nor competent in these areas. But it was part of the job, so even if it didn't feel comfortable, I did it.

Gardner Taylor: The most stressful time for me as a pastor was always Sunday morning at eleven o'clock. I loathed the time before the service, dreaded it. I would see people—street cleaners, for instance—and I'd envy them. I would wish that I could do what they were doing instead of what I had to do.

I would not see anyone after 10:30 a.m. People were very understanding that I needed this time alone. Then there was the long walk from my office back to my little room off of the sanctuary. That was always the longest walk of my week. Once I got started preaching, of course, it was different. At least it was most times. My mood and my spirit changed altogether once I got started. But the tension I experienced beforehand is something that most people don't understand. I've had people to say to me, "You do this so easily." They had no idea what I went through.

"WHAT I LIKED ABOUT MINISTRY"

Gardner Taylor: Although I dreaded the preaching ministry, it's also what I loved most. Once I got going on Sunday mornings, the nervousness that's almost inevitable got under control. I was delivered from it. I once asked my father, after he'd pastored over thirty years, "When do you get over the nervousness?" He replied, "I don't know." I ended up being a pastor a lot longer than he was, and I still don't know. But I'm convinced that the nervousness is a healthy thing, because it suggests that you're taking the preaching task very seriously. You're in a bad situation if you feel that your preaching doesn't make much difference.

But again, once I got into what I was trying to deal with that day, the nervousness turned into a sense of contentment, sometimes fulfillment. There was nothing in my week to compare with that. Sometimes it would be a sense of complete fulfillment, of feeling delivered by bearing the gospel, like a woman bearing a child.

Avery Lee: I prided myself in my preaching. I took it very seriously. I worked hard at it and always spent a lot of time preparing. I also felt that I was good at hospital visitation because I could listen well. For me, to go visit people was more than just a job. I really did care, and I think that that came through. I would always pray for healing, but healing doesn't always come. I would encourage others to be strengthened by their faith and to move on.

Young pastors ought to remember that they are in the pastorate largely because of a concern for people. This includes people who are sick and in hospitals. Even if nothing can be said or done, just a visit from a pastor can be very uplifting. It shows that you care. Pastors should never underestimate what this means to people.

COMMON MISTAKES OF PASTORS

Gardner Taylor: One mistake that a pastor sometimes makes is, whether in a sermon or in a conversation, talking to people as if he or she is from some exalted place beyond the reach of the common person. This kind of superciliousness, whereby a person seems to believe that ministers are of a different breed, turns people off.

Another mistake is wanting to impose upon people a vision without giving the people a chance to catch it. Nobody turns his or her life over to a stranger, and that's what a pastor is at the beginning of a ministry. Just the fact of being the minister does not guarantee that everyone is going to accept his or her word as being spoken *ex cathedra*, a word directly from God. One has to earn the right to be a pastor. The confidence of the people is something that has to be won. No piece of paper or official appointment from a bishop or vote of a congregation can take the place of winning the people's confidence.

THE ROLE OF HUMOR

Avery Lee: I advise younger pastors not to take themselves too seriously. As Paul said to the Romans, "I say to everyone among you to not think of yourself more highly than you ought" (Romans 12:3). If a sermon falls flat, it's not the end of the world or of your ministry. The pastoral life is full of pitfalls that make for humility. Instead of getting discouraged, embrace them as a way of following Paul's advice.

Yes, there will be times when the pastor encounters troubled waters. The bridge over these troubled waters is a sense of humor. Leslie Weatherhead writes in his book *This Is the Victory*, "Humor is one of the best solvents in the world for the grit of irritation that gets into the cogs of life these days, and the man who can laugh at himself as well as at others will be among the last casualties in the war of nerves."[1]

I have trouble trusting those who cannot laugh at themselves. Nothing more aptly suggests immaturity than the lack of a sense of humor. In fact, one of my pet peeves is the way that most artists have portrayed Jesus. Not only has Jesus been pictured as effeminate, but he is always serious and totally humorless. There's not even a twinkle in his eye. I believe that Jesus enjoyed life and had a keen sense of humor. I kept on my office wall a painting called *The Laughing Jesus*, by an artist whose name I cannot read. (It's the only such painting I've seen.)

No people in history have a deeper sense of humor than the Jews, despite their adversity. The ability of Jewish people to laugh at themselves and their circumstances might well be considered, almost literally, a saving grace.[2] There is an abundance of humor in the Bible in both Testaments. Is there any more mocking irony than what Elijah said to the priests of Baal on Mt. Carmel, "Cry a little louder!" when they were already shouting at the top of their lungs? Elijah taunted them that perhaps Baal had gone on a journey. The more literal Hebrew suggests, "Maybe he has gone to the toilet to relieve himself," but our modern translators have been more discreet.

Look at the New Testament. I find humor in the Pharisees sounding trumpets before them to announce that they are giving alms. And in that old busybody whose eye has a plank of lumber in it, but who is solicitous about the speck of dust in a neighbor's eye. And in that hypocrite who gags at a gnat of orthodoxy and then swallows a camel when it comes to personal practice.

Search for and find the humor in Jesus. Laughter rings around the world, and Galilee has its share. We can hear it. True, Jesus was "a man of sorrows and acquainted with grief." That means that his humor, his mirth, was consistent with a tender compassion for all that's frail. It was consistent also with profound reverence for all that's sublime in human life. But humor was far from absent in his ministry.

Why is it that certain conventions of Christianity have made both the Christian faith and its founder gloomy? Too many Christians have adopted the attitude that if anything is fun, it therefore must be sinful. Even Cruden, who gave us his famed concordance of the Bible, said, "To laugh is to be merry in a sinful manner." Who has more right to humor and fun, to feel joy in life, than the Christian, who knows, at least in theory, the source of what the Bible calls "joy unspeakable and full of glory"?

Christian faith makes room for the hard facts of life. It never minimizes the tragedy and sorrow. But Christian faith never despairs; it always hold out hope. When we can laugh, it means that the events around us have not gotten us down. In the midst of the world's raucous turmoil, a jubilant voice comes chiming through the centuries from a man standing by the shore of a lake in Galilee. The tribulation of the world is in his heart, but the laughter of heaven is in his eyes as he says, "Be of good cheer; I have overcome the world" (John 16:33, KJV).

PASTORAL COUNSELING

Avery Lee: The pastor as counselor must first be a good listener. A psychiatrist friend once told me that 85 percent of her patients only needed someone to listen for a while. It's the other 15 percent who need professional help. I love the title of the book *Listening with the Third Ear*,[3] that third ear being a sensitive antenna that can pick up the nuances of deeper-seated distress signals.

Pastors must recognize their limitations. Alexander Pope said, "A little knowledge is a dangerous thing." I entered the pastoral ministry with "a little knowledge" from a college major in psychology, plus some work in the psychiatry department of the Yale Medical School. I also had the ability to listen. So I thought I would be the ideal personal counselor.

Disillusionment came quickly. One of my first "counselees" was a young woman who was tied up in more knots than a ball of string. I could see quickly that I was in way over my head, and it became apparent that counseling was not to be my forte. Fortunately, I knew that an inexperienced counselor could do untold harm.

If someone came to me struggling with some aspect of their faith, perhaps experiencing doubts, I could handle that. Or if people were going through some of the common struggles that married couples experience, I could address that. But pastors need to err on the side of caution when it comes to counseling and consider making more referrals to trained experts. This is especially important in this day and age, when pastors are at risk of being sued for giving bad advice.

Also, the pastor must make sure that the counselor to whom he or she refers the counselee is competent. Not everyone who claims to be a personal counselor deserves that designation. I always felt that anyone who claims to be a "Christian counselor" merited an especially close look. It's one thing to be a counselor who's a Christian, but it seems presumptuous in this case to use "Christian" as an adjective.

The pastor must seek, find, and evaluate referral services. Listening and referring constitute good pastoral care. Also, pastors who have some training in the counseling area are well advised not to be so enamored with the analyst's couch that they neglect the church pew. Professional counseling and spiritual insight can work together to provide the healing and wholeness that people seek.

DIFFICULT PEOPLE

Gardner Taylor: Although I'm reluctant to say it, I truly believe that so-called difficult people in the church are, in a sense, almost given by God to keep the pastor humble. Such persons can be found in every congregation; they come with the church. The pastor's first job is to determine the cause or basis for the anger or frustration. Despite what might lie on the surface, most of the time the problem is not antagonism toward some church program or the pastor. Rather, there's something that lies underneath that causes this person to have a disagreeable disposition and attitude. Understanding this does not take away the burden of dealing with these people, but it does provide some sense of comfort and perspective. It is important for the minister to be polite, but sometimes it's necessary to be politely stern.

Avery Lee: Pastors will always have situations that they must address with regard to difficult people. It seems that every congregation has at least a few chronic naysayers. You just have to expect it and be ready. Certainly, the pastor cannot see such persons as an excuse to become callous or impolite in his or her own demeanor.

If there's conflict or deception being sown in the congregation, it becomes a priority to bring the facts and the truth out into the open. Those things that are hidden from the light are more likely to fester.

CHURCH DISCIPLINE

Gardner Taylor: Church discipline is appropriate when nothing else works. I view it as a last resort. The pastor ought to approach it with great reluctance, and the circumstances must clearly mandate it. It's something that should never be attempted unilaterally by a pastor.

The pastor must guard against becoming too personally involved in the issue or conflict. I advise calling together all the spiritual leaders of the congregation, whether they be deacons, deaconesses, elders, or leaders who hold some other title. Whatever decisions are made should be group decisions.

Avery Lee: I was aware that there were some people in the congregation who would have preferred another pastor. Not everybody's going to like the pastor. We got along at a distance.

In dealing with difficult people, I tried to be open and listen to their problems or criticisms, to take them under consideration. I tried to understand why they were the way they were. Were they like that with the former church leadership? If so, perhaps there's some underlying problem that needs to be addressed.

It's important for the pastor to be open to people, to listen, and to make every effort at reconciliation instead of alienation. But listening is not the same as being swayed.

CHOOSING BATTLES CAREFULLY

Avery Lee: In high school I was dating a girl. One night when I was at her house, the doorbell rang. The class bully was at the door challenging me to a fight. He said, "If she's worth having, she's worth fighting for, ain't she?" This guy would have beaten the living daylights out of me. So I answered, "Yes, she's worth fighting for, but right now I don't have to fight for her, because I have her." I closed the door and went back inside. (Later, he and I became friends—neither of us got the girl.)

My point is that some things are not worth fighting for. Sometimes, difficult people become difficult people because we allow them to instead of looking the other way. Certainly, some things *are* worth fighting for. But choose your battles carefully. I kept on my wall a poster that had on it the Latin phrase *Illigitimi non carborundum*, the literal translation of which is something like, "Do not let illicit, illogical, unsentimental persons wear you down." The more colorful translation is, "Don't let the ba—ds get you down."

PREACHING

Avery Lee: My main goal in preaching was to persuade at least one person who was listening to get more connected with God through faith in Christ. Although I would not consider my sermons evangelistic, many of them were geared for visitors. One of my regular themes was to challenge people to make a decision to do something for God. For some, that would mean coming to faith in Christ. For others, it might mean taking a significant step in demonstrating their faith. I was always hopeful of gaining new members for the church.

"SEEING" THE SCRIPTURE

Gardner Taylor: The goal of the pastor in preaching should be to "see" the Scripture. This means going far beyond merely reading and understanding the surface meaning. It entails searching for the profound and then exploring how it relates to the lives of the people. It entails opening up the amazing revelation in Scripture almost as a kind of mirror of what the people are going through.

Dr. Sandy Ray said that his greatest delight in his thirty-five years of ministry was "digging" for his people. It starts with digging. I found in my congregation that there was a great eagerness to hear, to understand, and to apply the gospel. It was not lost on me that I had an opportunity every week to influence people's lives. There's a mystery about this that cannot be described, and that mystery is the presence of the Holy Spirit and a kind of seizure of one's personality that I think no one can put into words.

"STAND FOR SOMETHING"

Avery Lee: Pastors who try to keep everybody happy with their preaching typically end up not saying much of anything and sometimes not keeping anybody happy. I was never a fire-and-brimstone preacher, but I still like the illustration of the mythological preacher who is reported to have said, "You must repent, as it were, and be converted, more or less, or you will be damned, to some extent." The point is that good preaching is ambitious and sometimes takes risks.

Preaching that avoids or tiptoes around the important issues of the day is destined for irrelevance. Preachers should not engage in controversy for its own sake, but neither should they try to avoid controversial preaching. Walking this tightrope can be difficult, particularly if the congregation is divided, perhaps over the country's decision to go to war, or maybe over a local labor dispute.

I think that the most challenging period for me with respect to preaching was in the 1960s during the Vietnam War and the civil rights movement. With the war, young people were being killed; families were being shattered. I'm sure that people in my congregation knew that I opposed the war, but for the most part, my sermons were not for or against. I focused on the healing of emotions and on hope. When it came to issues related to civil rights and desegregation, I was far more ambitious, far less guarded. Ours was a church that welcomed all people, regardless of the color of their skin.

If preaching is to be prophetic, I don't know that it's possible to avoid the feeling that you're taking sides with respect to politics. My congregation knew that I was a "Yellow Dog Democrat." Some of them were Republicans. They just said, "We'll let Avery be wrong." There were times when some in the congregation wanted to run me out of town. To his credit, on one occasion the chairman of the deacons said to the congregation, "We might not like what Avery preaches, but he has a right to say it." You might say that they allowed me the privilege of being wrong.

Preachers who aspire to be prophetic must do their best to make sure that their words of challenge are addressed to the powers that be across the political and social spectrums. Even with this, some will accuse you of taking sides, and to some extent they are correct. But you've got to be true to yourself and proclaim what you believe based on your own study and spirituality. Some people will leave the church because of it, but others might come.

KEEPING IT SIMPLE

Avery Lee: The pulpit is not the place for pastors to display their brilliance. Brilliant people can mumble a vocabulary laced with technical terms that can make listeners feel like fools. We can talk about "dynamically interfacing so as to impact and conceptualize our paradigms," or instead we can say, "Let's talk about it and see what we can do." People want to hear about the good news of the gospel in terms that they can understand.

THE STRESS OF PREACHING IN PERSPECTIVE

Gardner Taylor: Earlier, I noted the stress associated with preaching. I know I'm not alone in this. I've talked with many preachers who have this same dread. I've done a lot of public speaking at dinner events and prayer breakfasts. That presents no stress for me at all, because it's not a worship service. I've pondered a thousand times why there should be a difference. And I don't know if I can explain it. It's a mystery. The nearest I can come is to say that there is a monumental difference between talking to people about their affairs (after-dinner speaking) and talking to them about God. Declaring to people the things of God is accompanied by a kind of pressure that's absent at an after-dinner speech.

As I've stated, once I started preaching, I would be fine. Often the result would be a sense of fulfillment. But even in these times, by Tuesday or Wednesday I would realize how fragmentary, how fractional, my effort had been. And so I would go back and try again. And so I did. Each Sunday I had the opportunity to reach as many as two thousand people. To send them out of there by God's grace with some sense of purpose, or feeling comforted and encouraged—that was my highest goal and my biggest challenge as a pastor.

DEVELOPING PREACHING SKILLS

Avery Lee: There's a bit of "ham actor" in every preacher. There's more of it in some—including me—than in others. Some preachers are natural-born orators; others of us have to work at it.

In his younger days a friend of mine would go off into the woods and read aloud the Bible, great poetry, and Shakespeare in order to develop the cadence and beauty of the spoken word. I'm sure that this practice made my friend—Gardner Taylor—a more effective preacher. Others would do well to emulate him in this regard.

Many readers of this book, no doubt, have had classes on the preparation and delivery of sermons, classes taught by competent professors who used good textbooks. So did I. But the best advice I ever heard and applied came not from a professor of homiletics, but from the teacher of a creative writing class at the University of Oklahoma. In a seminar on writing nonfiction articles for magazines, he gave a four-word formula that I used from that point on in my preaching: "Hey! You. See. So." "Hey" to get their attention. "You" to make it personal. "See" as in "This is what I'm talking about." And "So" as in "What are you going to do about it?" Every sermon ought to have all four of these elements.

Another way to improve sermon skills is to take on a "designated listener." In my early years I delivered a sermon in which I used a phrase and explained what it meant "in the original Greek." After church, a woman introduced herself and said she was a professor of classical Greek at the local university. "You used the Greek especially well this morning," she said. Despite the compliment, a lightbulb flashed in my head that warned, "Be careful what you say; chances are that someone out there will know more about it than you do." Thus the need for a designated listener.

A designated listener is, in essence, a friendly critic. During most of my years in ministry, I had a designated listener. (If a baseball team can have a designated hitter, why can't a pastor have a designated listener?) This listener should be someone known only to the two of you, not by the congregation. Of course, it must be someone you can trust to "tell it like it is." In one church my designated listener was a female English literature professor at Louisiana Tech. In another church it was a traveling salesman who was a voracious reader with vast knowledge.

In addition to content, a good designated listener can watch for grammar, pronunciation, and factual accuracy and can even make suggestions to improve the sermon delivery. Pastors who are willing to invite such critique must make a commitment to themselves not to pout upon hearing things they might not want to hear. Instead, they should be grateful for the help.

PREACHING IN A TIME OF COMMUNITY OR NATIONAL TRAGEDY

Gardner Taylor: It's important in one's preaching to find the right balance between not minimizing what has happened, on the one hand, while not overplaying it, on the other. Ultimately, the preacher ought to proclaim that regardless of what has happened, God is not dead, and out of the worst set of circumstances, God works his mercy.

God's goodness may not be seen immediately. There's a large place for doubt, even anger, at God. It's not unreasonable or unrighteous to be angry with God. In fact, I believe that it's a false piety that removes God's presence from our emotions. It's artificial. But doubt, frustration, and anger are not permanent states. The gospel proclaims the promises of God, promises full of hope, mercy, and love.

SERMON PREPARATION

Gardner Taylor: I do not recommend this approach to young pastors, but the reality is that I moved on what Alexander Maclaren used to call "very narrow margins of reserve." This is to say that I hardly knew on the Monday preceding the coming Sunday what I was going to preach about. Strangely enough, by Tuesday evening most weeks, I would begin to have some faint idea what I was going to deal with. Often it related to things that I read in the newspaper or heard from people. I wrote my sermons out in longhand. After dinner on Friday I would write until I was satisfied with what I was going to preach about. Sometimes I would write until I saw the dawn; I never felt comfortable waking up on Saturday without having the sermon finished.

Avery Lee: When I first started preaching, I preached from an outline. I'd done some preaching prior to going to seminary, mostly at a rural church in West Texas, and I'd always preached from an outline. At seminary, it came my turn to preach in a homiletics class. After I finished my extemporaneous sermon from an outline, Professor Halford Luccock said to me, "Mr. Lee, what you said, you said very well. You just didn't have much to say." The wind was taken out of my sermon sails. Professor Luccock set me to the task of writing my sermons out in full. He said to try it for a year. I did, and I never stopped.

First I'd write the sermon out in longhand. Then someone would type it for me. I did most of my sermon preparation in the mornings. People in the congregation knew that this was the time I was not to be disturbed, except for urgent matters. Sometimes I would think about or work on sermons during hospital visitation or an administrative committee meeting. In both cases, there was frequently lots of downtime. I now have in a closet over fifty years' worth of written sermons, all of which take about twenty-two minutes to preach.

But when you're preaching from a manuscript, it's important not to lose the sense of extemporaneous delivery. Don't just bury your head while reading. You need to know what you've written well enough to be flexible. Don't stare down at your manuscript or look only in one direction. Keep eye contact with the people.

Once I was asked to speak at a pastors' retreat. The place was a campground facility. It was night. Just as I stood up to begin, every light on the campground went out. It was almost total darkness. I delivered the sermon without missing anything important, even though I did some extemporizing. I did not relish this experience, but it did convince me of the importance of knowing well what you're going to say before you get up to say it.

Gardner Taylor: Even though I wrote my sermons, I didn't use a manuscript in the pulpit. Writing the sermon gave me a good sense of where I was going and of terminology. I read through the sermon two or three times on Saturday and on Sunday morning. Sometimes at breakfast on Sunday, I'd still be making changes. Laura would say to me, "If you don't have it by now, you won't get it," but I made revisions anyway.

Even though I didn't use the manuscript, early in my ministry I still took it with me to the pulpit. Once Laura asked me, "Why are you taking it up there if you're not going to use it?" So I took her advice. For the first three or four minutes, I missed it. But then I got going, and I haven't taken a manuscript into the pulpit since.

All my sermons were about thirty minutes in length. I knew that ten or eleven pages of my own scribbling was about the right length. I also had what the jockeys call "a clock in the head." That is to say that a good jockey knows when to "rate" the horse, which means to increase the speed near the finish line. I had that kind of sense in the pulpit. I could almost always feel the sermon coming to its natural conclusion.

ON BORROWING

Avery Lee: When Leslie Weatherhead delivered the Lyman Beecher Lectures on preaching at Yale, Professor Halford Luccock introduced him by saying something like, "I have read his sermon books, and they are good. I have preached his sermons, and, lo, they are very good." Another of my professors advised, "Remember, all work and no plagiarism makes Jack a dull preacher."

What I'm saying is that there's nothing wrong with borrowing material from others. What's important is to give proper credit. There's a sense in which it's all been said before, but it's up to the preacher to find a way to say it differently. Or as still another professor put it, "Every pastor must graze in someone else's pasture, but he must chew his own cud."

IDEAS FOR SERMON CONTENT

Gardner Taylor: I was in the habit of jotting down pretty much anything and everything that came to me as an idea for a sermon. For example, I had the practice of writing in the flyleaf of books ideas for sermons or material that could feed into a sermon. I also got a lot of ideas from the theater. My first wife was a lover of the theater, and so is my second wife, so a great many ideas came from Broadway.

Of course, I got ideas mainly from the Bible. Once when I

was preaching in Louisville, I heard a preacher by the name of J. B. Bottoms make the statement "No one ought to live without reading through the entire Bible at least once." Well, I had never done that, so I decided I would. Each morning I read a chapter from the Old Testament and from the New Testament. Sometimes ideas would leap out of the pages and get hold of me and shake me.

I read the *New York Times* every day. So many things would turn up, sometimes hidden in a standard news article. For example, I recall an article about a man who lived in a $700,000 house and who shot himself to death while he was in his Mercedes Benz. That says something about our culture of materialism.

Reading a daily newspaper helps to keep your preaching current. You have to be careful not to preach exclusively from the morning press. And you also have to be careful not to preach—and I state this advisedly—exclusively from Scripture. You've got to bring the two together.

I don't know whether it's vain imagining, but very frequently I was almost startled at the way the Scriptures addressed current events and at the way current events addressed Scripture. It helped me appreciate even more the fact that the Bible is a living book; it has a life of its own. It runs the gamut of the human experience.

Avery Lee: Even though I didn't follow the lectionary, I recognize that it's a good tool for ensuring that preachers cover a wide range of the Bible's themes and topics. For those who do not follow the lectionary, here are some ideas that could assist the congregation in becoming better acquainted with the whole Bible while allowing the preacher to set forth his or her thinking and interpretation. One could preach on the personalities of the prophets; the "first family" (Adam, Eve, Cain, Abel); faith's "founding fathers" (and "mothers") from both the Old and the New Testaments; or early church fathers such as Augustine, Luther, and Calvin. One could develop a series of sermons based on key figures in his or her church's denominational history.

Other ideas for sermon series include the parables of Jesus; what Jesus said about himself (the "I Am" statements); the Ten Commandments (no, they are not out of date); the Sermon on the Mount; the Seven Deadly Sins; the Seven Virtues; the Seven Last Words from the Cross. I have done a sermon series based on questions that God or Jesus asked: "Adam, Where Are You?"; "Cain, Where Is Your Brother?"; "Moses, What's in Your Hand?"; "Isaiah, Whom Shall I Send?"; "Elijah, What Are You Doing Here?"; "Jonah, Why Are You So Angry?"; "Pharisees, What Do You Think of Christ?"; "Peter, Do You Love Me?"

Don't overlook sources other than the Bible for inspiration. Consider drama: William Shakespeare, Eugene O'Neil, Neil Simon, Tennessee Williams, Thornton Wilder, and many more. And Broadway musicals. In *Fiddler on the Roof*, Tevye's lament "Why my horse?" sounds a lot like Job. The theme of grace is central to *Les Miserables*. One might not agree with all the theology in *Jesus Christ Superstar*, but it's hard not to be moved by Mary Magdalene's "I Don't Know How to Love Him" or Jesus' (in Gethsemane) "If There Is a Way."

I've preached sermons based on popular songs, such as Louis Armstrong's "What a Wonderful World." I preached a series of sermons on country songs that were printed in the book *Take Me Home, Country Road*. The point is that a little imagination goes a long way.

Gardner Taylor: I got many wonderful ideas from the theater. One that stands out is a Civil War–era play in which a man is being tried for cruelty to the prisoners. The man defends himself by saying that he was merely following orders. But the judge responds by saying, "Whoever is a member of the human race is elected to an extraordinary responsibility." This is just one small example of the kind of thing I would work into a sermon to make the point that as human beings, and especially as Christians, we are responsible for one another.

PREACHING FROM A BOOK OF THE BIBLE

Gardner Taylor: In the last years of my ministry, I did something that I highly recommend, with some caveats. I preached for over a year on the book of Ephesians, and then for three years from the book of Revelation. This kind of sequential preaching can be very meaningful. But it's difficult, and it can even be daunting going week after week, verse by verse. You may not feel like doing it, but it's a good discipline. It forces you to examine each verse very thoroughly. I found that as I dug into the book, many things would surface, and one thing would suggest another. Sometimes I spent more than one week on a single verse or passage because the content demanded it.

PREACHING AS ART

Gardner Taylor: I credit Paul Scherer with helping to bring to fruition whatever native gift I had for imaginativeness that grew out of my own black background. He was the pastor of the Holy Trinity Lutheran Church in Manhattan. He had a kind of feeling for Scripture that enabled him to see the people and events of Scripture with a sense of imagination. It was a tremendous gift.

Scherer also had a feeling for language, which is the main weaponry a preacher has. I still recall the story told by a man who went on to teach preaching at Lutheran Seminary. This man, Harold Albert, had applied for an assistantship at Holy Trinity and came to the church to meet Scherer. The pastor's secretary told him that Pastor Scherer was busy. Harold could see into the office and could tell that the pastor was not meeting with anyone, nor was he on the phone. He could see Scherer's arm swinging backward and forward. When Albert finally went in, Scherer said to him, "I'm sorry to have kept you waiting, but I was trying to think of a word."

I urge all preachers to take a single word most seriously. I think that we have seen in preaching in general a sort of de-poeticizing of the language as part of an effort to "dumb down" the content, to make it simple. People don't want to be dumbed down; they want to be lifted up. In this regard, I think that we need to recover a sense of preaching as an art form, one that features grand and piercing language, language that wrestles with and grips the hearer.

STUDY

Gardner Taylor: Many pastors underestimate the riches to be found in the Scriptures. Seeking the meaning and relevance of the Scriptures for us today is no simple task. It's something that must be sought. Today we are dealing with the temptation always to simplify. In seeking to understand and apply Scripture, we have to recover our imaginativeness. Not everything is metallic, flat-topped. I'm not advising people to make everything murky in the name of intellectuality, because I believe that profound truths are simple truths, truths people can recognize. But even simple truths must be uncovered through sincere effort.

Avery Lee: It's been said that Harry Emerson Fosdick spent one hour of preparation for each minute that he preached. Anyone who heard him or has read his sermons has no trouble believing that this is true. This requires strict discipline, designating time for study, whether in your office or at home.

One pastor I know had his office at one place in the church and a study at another place in the church. He decided to give his study a name. He called it "The Hospital in Monroe, Louisiana." Anytime he was in his study and someone called the church to ask for him, the secretary would say, "He's at the hospital in Monroe. He'll be back at his office at one o'clock this afternoon."

Nearly seventy years ago, on the last day of a class in modern poetry, W. D. Bond, a professor of English literature at Hardin-Simmons University, said something that I wrote on the flyleaf of a textbook and have taken to heart through the years: "Never give up the search for knowledge and truth. Never stop learning." For the pastor, this means continuing education. You may have graduated from a theological seminary, and you may even have a Ph.D., but still, the educational process never ceases. Opportunities today are virtually limitless, especially for those who live near a university or seminary. These range from day-long seminars to night courses to full-fledged Doctor of Ministry programs. And of course, many good opportunities are available today over the Internet. (Or so I've heard. In my case, the computer revolution proved that there are some new tricks that an old dog will never learn!)

Pastors ought to suggest that the budget committee include funds for continuing education. They should also encourage their congregation to be open to the pastor taking leaves of absence for the purpose of study. I might suggest an extended leave of two or three months every three or four years.

Gardner Taylor: You can't talk with avid golfers more than ten or fifteen minutes before they start talking about Walter Hagen or

Bobby Jones. Or with baseball fans without hearing them talk about Ted Williams and Babe Ruth. I find it very sad that in the theological arena, studying the great ideas and preachers of the past is looked upon with little regard. I've taught at seminaries and discovered that these young people know nothing about the people of the past. Sometimes, even those who teach them don't know.

ON READING

Avery Lee: Dante described hell as "that day when we read no more." At age seventy-seven I was stricken with an eye infection. For two months I couldn't read. Dante was right. How else can we sample and know the surges of life unless we share the thoughts and experiences of others, past and present? Now, in my ninth decade of life, I continue to read as much as ever, perhaps more.

Beyond technical biblical, theological, and homiletical works, a pastor needs to read fiction, nonfiction biographies, drama, musical plays, poetry, and magazines. Even "Dear Abby" columns help to put clergy in touch with people. The pastor needs to know what's going on in the world outside the church and religion.

To the person who says, "But I just don't have time for all that reading," I say, "Bosh!" When a pastor is through reading, that pastor is through, period. A person who really wants to read will find the time. Carry a book in your pocket. A lot of time is wasted while waiting around to see people—in a doctor's office, for example.

RECOMMENDED BOOKS

Avery Lee: If I were to build a personal library and had a thousand dollars to spend, here's what I would include:

■ As many different translations of the Bible as I could acquire.

■ One or more good Bible concordances. I like *Young's Analytical Concordance to the Bible* (Thomas Nelson Publishers).

■ Bible dictionaries. The five-volume *Interpreter's Dictionary of the Bible* (Abingdon Press) is expensive but comprehensive.

■ Bible commentaries. My favorite is the twelve-volume *Interpreter's Bible* (Abingdon Press).[1]

■ A Bible atlas.

■ *Roget's Thesaurus.*

■ Books of poetry, plays, and quotations. I suggest Bergen Evans's *Dictionary of Quotations* (Delacorte Press); *The Oxford Book of English Verse*, edited by Arthur Quiller-Couch (Clarendon Press); *Modern American and British Poetry*, edited by Louis Untermeyer (Harcourt, Brace & Company); and the complete works of William Shakespeare.

■ Historic sermons from preachers such as Fosdick, Weatherhead, Spurgeon, Sockman, and Bonnell. Clyde Fant's thirteen-volume *20 Centuries of Great Preaching* (Word Books) fits the bill here.

■ Service books. I recommend *Minister's Service Book for Pulpit and Parish*, edited by James Dalton Morrison (Willett, Clark & Company). The Anglican Church's *Book of Common Prayer* is something I've used for over five hundred weddings. (The days of people writing their own wedding ceremony seem to have ended—thank goodness!) A useful resource for funerals is *A Service Book* (published by the National Selected Morticians), and probably you can get a complimentary copy from your local funeral home.

■ Fiction—lots of fiction.

Gardner Taylor: The pastor ought to have ready access to a complete, good encyclopedia set. There are many things that a pastor will have to research.

I also highly recommend resources that get a pastor in touch with the great preachers of the past, preachers such as Joseph Parker, Reinhold Niebuhr, Charles Spurgeon, Paul Scherer, Peter Taylor Forsyth, and Harry Emerson Fosdick. I think that one ought to pick up this kind of material to catch a sense of how great preachers from the somewhat recent past have dealt with the gospel.

For many years I was not moved by Spurgeon. But once,

while I was preaching in Australia, I met a man, Mervin Himbry, who would become a dear friend. He put me on to Spurgeon again, and I began reading him. I found that not everything was a gem, but in the midst of some dullness, I discovered a lot of treasure. Spurgeon had a tremendous wit, and I think that's important. Spurgeon once was told that a man had said something very unpleasant about him. Spurgeon's response was, "He said that because he did not know me. If he'd have known me, he would have said something much worse."

Many years ago I was deeply disappointed and hurt as a result of having to break with the National Baptist Convention. I spent much of that winter reading, of all things, Paul Tillich's trilogy in systematic theology, difficult Germanic constructions and all. I gained enormously from that, not just intellectually, but also spiritually. Tillich was, in the best sense of the word, a "sophisticated" theologian. He had a grasp of the arts and literature, and he had a strong sense of the currents that run through society. His was not, in the negative sense of the word, a "pietistic" kind of rendering. The divine truth that he revealed came partly from a secularist point of view.

Pastors will be greatly enriched for going back and reading Reinhold Niebuhr, because truth as he put it forth is ageless. And young pastors need to come to know Peter Taylor Forsyth. His biographers said that he was a difficult guest in a house, but the children of the house loved him. It was Forsyth who said, "I do not believe in the literal inspiration of Scripture, but I find the Scripture addressing every need so directly that I find it difficult not to believe." And he spoke of preaching as a "prolongation of the gospel." This man had amazing insights.

Pastors should read Joseph Parker, because those English preachers had something that has been lost. They had not only a strong grasp of Scripture, but also a vividness of expression. Parker exhibited an imaginativeness that our contemporary culture discourages in the interest of flat-topped reasoning.

Pastors should read Henry Ward Beecher, a preacher of abolitionism who pastored in Brooklyn. Beecher had an enormous social passion. He engaged the America of his time in relating the Scripture to what was going on. The preacher's job, after all, is to get the ancient out of the past and into the present. Beecher had a gift for that.

Harry Emerson Fosdick had a similar gift. In an age when a simplistic and narrow kind of fundamentalism was taking over, Fosdick stood for an expression of faith that did not reject the new science, but rather incorporated it into the gospel. His preaching was tremendously significant. His critics have not seen his deep reverence for the faith and for the Scriptures, though he did not view them slavishly.

There are also many contemporary works that come to mind. Lately, just as an actor tries to get inside a character, I've been trying to get inside the mind of the apostle Paul. Luke Johnson at Emory University has been most helpful in this regard.

When it comes to preaching, Fred Craddock has a pert way of putting things, and the result is some dazzling insights. Also, I consider Samuel Proctor's book *The Certain Sound of the Trumpet* the finest resource on preaching that's been done in at least fifty years.

LIMITING THE EXPENSE

Avery Lee: I realize that books are expensive, but there are many ways to minimize the expense. Use public and school libraries. Talk with the finance committee about putting a "book allowance" line item in the church budget. Talk with other pastors about book sharing. (But *never* put marks in a book that isn't yours!) When it comes to fiction, learn which members of your congregation are fiction readers, and then establish a "lending library." Look for bargains in bookstores that sell used books. Join a book club and get four books for a dollar; then buy the required additional books, quit, and join another club. Find a retired minister in the area who might be willing to part with some of his or her library. Get acquainted and ask.

EXPANDING HORIZONS

Avery Lee: Some pastors build a library that reinforces their own views and positions. They never read anything that would challenge or upset them. A fairly well-known pastor once said to me, "Avery, I never read any of the new books on theology or biblical studies. They might upset my faith." I brashly replied, "If your faith is that weak, perhaps it needs to be upset."

Many years ago I borrowed Karl Marx's *Das Kapital* from the library at Louisiana Tech. Someone learned about it and began spreading the news that I was a communist! After all, I'd checked out Marx's book and was reading it. My name was the only one on the check-out slip. Alas, they didn't accuse the library of being communist for having the book on its shelves.

CHURCH ADMINISTRATION

Gardner Taylor: Part of the administrative task is leadership. I believe that effective leaders set goals for the congregation that can be reached but are not easily attainable. This approach builds confidence while stretching the church to reach its full potential. These goals should be developed and espoused in light of the gospel.

Avery Lee: My guess is that many, if not most, pastors struggle in the area of church administration. This isn't surprising. People respond to a call to ministry out of a desire to preach and provide pastoral care, not to preside over business meetings or worry about church finances.

People expect a lot of their pastor. Most pastors expect a lot of themselves. But we all have our limitations—our strengths and weaknesses. No pastor is competent in every area of ministry. Some are better at pastoral care than they are at preaching, or vice versa. But it's important for the pastor at least to recognize his or her own areas of giftedness. I believe that pastors should exercise their strengths and work on their weaknesses.

Although weaknesses should be recognized, they should not be permitted to serve as blanket excuses or as a way of avoiding the responsibilities that come with pastoral leadership, including in the area of church administration. President Harry Truman's desk motto, "The buck stops here," is true for the pastor as well.

Even if you serve a church that is large and affluent enough to have a staff member serve as administrator, you are still to be the chief administrator, the person with whom "the buck stops."

Gardner Taylor: I was blessed through my years in pastoral ministry to have extraordinary people who handled the day-to-day business of the congregation, people who had a penchant for details. My administrative assistant for thirty-five years, Wyatt Logan, was typically at the office at seven o'clock in the morning, and sometimes he would stay until late at night. The pastor does well to find such people.

I recall from my youth a New Orleans businessman and devout layman named James G. Gayle who used to say, "A good executive is not somebody who can do ten men's work, but somebody who has sense enough to find ten men to do the work."

Most congregations have people—including businesspeople and bookkeepers—who are thoroughly capable and willing but who need to be identified and encouraged to serve in this way.

ADMINISTRATIVE STYLE

Gardner Taylor: The best cure for infection is sunlight. And so it's important for the pastor who wants to be an effective administrator to keep things out in the open. Don't let anything be hidden.

Avery Lee: When it comes to managing the affairs of the church, there are two extremes. One extreme is to be a "control freak," someone who has to know everything that's going on or being planned. This pastor imposes his or her will to make sure that everything is done just the right way. The other extreme, of course, is a pastor who has no idea about what's going on in the church.

As with so many other areas, when it comes to managing the church, it's important to find a balance between a "hands on" and a "hands off" approach. It's important to know what's being planned but also to allow the people who are responsible to go ahead on their own. After all, the choral director probably knows more about music than you do, and the director of Christian education knows more about curriculum materials. So meet and plan together, but then give others the freedom to exercise their gifts.

The first pastor with whom I worked as an associate pastor was a control freak of the highest order. He had to know about everything, be a part of everything, and get it done his way. A pastor like that is certain to stifle creativity and to diminish initiative.

The second pastor with whom I worked took a different approach. When he asked me to become his associate, he said,

"Avery, if we didn't think you had sense enough to do this job, we wouldn't have asked you to do it! If you need me, ask." Of course, he knew what was going on, but he left me and others on the staff alone to get it done. In naval terms, he "ran a loose ship."

When I became a pastor, the path of the second man became my role model, partly because it fit my personality. I sat in on planning meetings, speaking out when I was asked or when I thought it necessary to interject my opinions. Some people thought that I ran too loose a ship. But things got done, and for the most part, harmoniously.

Pastors who are tempted to be overly controlling need to remember that they, like those who sit in their pews, are ultimately human beings who are capable of being wrong, sometimes very wrong. Thus, it's important to consider other perspectives. I recall the early advice I received as an associate pastor from one of my mentors who said, "Avery, when two people always agree, one of them isn't thinking." To consider the perspectives of others is a sign not of weakness, but of wisdom.

Where a pastor lands on the control-freedom continuum will depend in part on his or her personality and style. I caution against imposing your stubborn will, although there are times when you must take a stand. The old saying "Stand for something lest you fall for anything" is true for the pastor. But choose only those battles that are worth fighting for.

Gardner Taylor: My theory of pastoring was this: "If it didn't look to me like it would hurt anything, I'd say go ahead and do it." There was a woman in my congregation, Myrtle Braithwaite, who was a social worker by profession. Almost every ministry that Concord Church carried on, including the nursing home, came out of her head.

If somebody has an idea, the pastor ought to weigh the pros and cons. The same is true when the pastor has an idea. He or she needs another viewpoint. And it must be an honest viewpoint. I am reminded of a line from a play: "They do abuse the king that flatter him."

In sum, every idea should be brought to the marketplace of discussion, debate, and refinement. Look at both the potential problems and the possibilities. But if I didn't see any clear-cut negatives, I'd say, "Let's go." And then I would support the effort in whatever way I could.

FINANCIAL ISSUES

Gardner Taylor: The pastor's primary responsibility in the area of finances and stewardship is to provide biblical instruction, not only with respect to what the congregation ought to be doing, but also with regard to attitude. People ought to give not grudgingly, but willingly.

I didn't discuss issues related to money and stewardship as

much as I might have, so I don't hold myself up as a model in this area. Pastors need to talk about money, not just for the good of the church, but mainly for the good of the people. People who don't give are deprived of a blessing. This is especially important in light of our culture's predisposition toward materialism. Genuine blessings come not from things, but from sharing what we have to help others and to advance God's kingdom.

The Seventh Day Adventist preacher E. E. Mims once came to Concord as a guest lecturer, and what he had to say changed the course of the church's giving. He pictured a tray of ten apples and represented God as saying, "All these apples are mine. You are not able to make an apple of your own. But you can have all of these apples. All I ask is that you return one to me so I can make more." Before long, Concord Church had an endowment of a million dollars, which became the Concord Christ Fund, out of which community projects were supported by interest from the fund.

WEDDINGS AND FUNERALS

PREMARITAL COUNSELING

Avery Lee: I didn't do a lot of premarital counseling, because most of the people in the church whom I married I already knew very well. Of course, the pastor will have many situations in which he or she is approached by couples outside the church who want to be married in a church in order to receive the blessing of the church. I tried to use these situations as opportunities to get people back to the church, to get reconnected—or perhaps connected for the first time—with God.

Some situations were very difficult. There were times when I married people who I wasn't sure ought to be married. I did it because I knew they were dead set on getting married anyway, and I wanted to do what I could to help the marriage succeed. This was my approach when I had some doubts, some uncertainty. There were other times when I had not just doubts, but strong reservations. I don't recall ever telling anyone, "I'm not going to do this because you're never going to make it." But in these cases I referred the couple to a professional counselor, to someone in a better position than I was in to help them decide whether to marry and to better understand the challenges that they might anticipate.

Gardner Taylor: When I began in pastoral ministry, the value of counseling was not as greatly understood and appreciated as it is today. I typically performed some fifty weddings a year—nearly one a week. One of my associates would talk to the people. I wasn't coldhearted or uncaring, but by the time they got to me, it was almost just a ceremony.

I think that counseling is very important, but I didn't do much of it. I wish I had. Of course, I or one of my associates spoke with couples. But by and large we didn't delve very deeply into the issues that all couples ought to consider before getting married. There were times when I was unsure that a particular marriage ought to be taking place.

I think that churches ought to have a formal policy with regard to premarital counseling. Ours did not have one. Frankly, I consider this one of the weaker parts of my ministry.

FUNERALS

Avery Lee: A funeral is just as singular an event as a baptism or a marriage, so the pastor ought to make it personal. This is easy to do if the deceased is someone the pastor knew for a long time. But if a pastor is new to the church, or if the deceased was not well connected with the church, the pastor will not know much about the person's life—the person's loves, interests, activities, favorite hymns and Scriptures. In such cases the pastor should not be shy about speaking with family members and friends to learn more about the deceased. Those who are grieving often find it therapeutic to talk about their loved one.

I recall the example of Rabbi Edward Cohn, who had been rabbi at Temple Sinai in New Orleans for only a few days when one of the prominent members died. When he spoke at her funeral, you would have thought he'd known her all her life. He had taken the time to be with the family and friends to learn as much as possible so as to make the service personal.

DIFFICULT FUNERALS

Gardner Taylor: The pastor occasionally is called upon to officiate at a funeral for someone for whom it may be hard to find kind words. What is the pastor to say? My father had an answer to this question. He talked about the preacher who had to do a funeral for someone in town. This preacher was known for saying something favorable about everyone. The deceased was known as someone about whom no one had anything good to say. Everyone in this little town attended the funeral at the church to hear what the preacher had to say. The preacher spoke: "Mr. Jones was not as bad sometimes as he was at other times."

The goal is to etch out something positive about a life. A funeral is not a time for condemnation. It is not a time for lying either, because a pastor's credibility is on the line. It can be a fine line, but this is a time for the pastor to accentuate the positive and to provide comfort and hope for the living.

My successor at Concord, Gary Simpson, is very good at this. He is almost generous. He is able to find common ground in humanity with the deceased and to examine the person's life in the light of God's mercy and love. He has the gift of finding becoming aspects of humor the deceased possessed. It's an approach that all pastors should emulate.

Avery Lee: By far, the toughest funeral is for someone who committed suicide. This is something I faced on only two or three occasions, but it is very difficult, partly because those who are living may feel guilty.

Hard as it is, it's important to find something positive, something encouraging. I think that it's helpful to talk first about what we do not know, and then to talk about what we do know. We do not know exactly what happened, what the person may have been going through. Obviously, something happened that the person couldn't handle, couldn't sort out. But we can't know what the person may have been thinking or feeling, including about God.

On the other hand, we do know that ours is a God of mercy and compassion. I didn't preach hell—fire and brimstone. As much as I wanted people to come to Christ and tried to make that happen, I didn't feel comfortable determining what happens when someone dies outside the church. I don't believe that we can know that. We can pray and we can hope, but this is up to a loving God.

HUMOR

Avery Lee: I have always believed there is place for humor at a funeral service. I recall one woman from our church, a feminist with a great sense of humor, whose life was taken by cancer. At her memorial service I pictured her being welcomed to heaven. The angel Gabriel was there with a trumpet fanfare. St. Paul took over with some abstractions about "this mortal must take on the immortal." The new arrival couldn't take it any longer, so she spoke up: "Now, Paul," she said—not "sainting" him— "you just wait a minute. We have time here, lots of time, so they tell me, and there are some things I want to tell you about you saying that some of your best friends were women. Oh, I know about Lydia and the others. But in fact, you did a lot of harm to the women of my day. Maybe some of us misunderstood what you wrote. That's easy enough to do, especially for some preachers I know who are so insecure that they feel threatened by women and are afraid that they'll take over the church. Well, if we women hadn't done some of the things we did, the church would be in worse shape than it is. But we'll talk about that later."

Then there was the funeral of a friend who was an avid golfer, although he wasn't very good at the game. His body was cremated. His final request was that his ashes be spread in a sand trap, because that's where his shots landed most of the time. Then, whenever his friends hit a shot out of that sand trap, they would be hitting a piece of him. At his memorial service, I made sure to convey his wishes.

Humor reinforces our confidence that for the Christian, death is not the end. It's the beginning of a more meaningful life. We have God's assurance that eternal life is a gift of God. The funeral service must make this assurance central, and humor can help.

SELF-CARE

Gardner Taylor: Much of the pastor's time and energy is spent accomplishing the tasks associated with professional ministry. There's nothing wrong with that, but every minister ought to cultivate relationships with people with whom he or she can sit down and be real and natural, without having to wear a mask.

I can understand how easy it is for a person in pastoral ministry to throw up his or her hands in despair. It's the kind of work that you never finish. No matter how long you're at it, at the last hour you realize that there's something else you should have seen, something else you should have said or done.

I was blessed throughout my ministry with other pastors and with officers in my congregation who were very kind to me, who lifted me up before God, and who nurtured me. Pastors need people, whether inside or outside the congregation, to whom they can turn for advice or support when they need it. When I was young, I viewed these men as fathers. When they were gone, others replaced them whom I considered brothers. In my later years I viewed some of these friends and supporters as sons. And I've always had a wonderful relationship with one or two pastors along the way.

Avery Lee: People in the congregation need to understand that pastors are people too. Pastors have lives beyond the church. People should give pastors the freedom to live their lives. They should not confuse pastors with perfect people. We are altogether as human as everyone else.

I always had people in the church whom I considered close friends. The pastor needs to have people with whom to share ideas, thoughts, and struggles. They don't have to be church members. It could be someone at the local Kiwanis Club, or perhaps another pastor from the local federation of churches. Pastors who don't have such relationships should make it a priority to form them.

Gardner Taylor: The pastor would not say it bluntly, of course, but he or she must find ways to communicate this message to the congregation: "Leave me alone." I don't think that you can do that in a day or even in a year. It takes time for people to be directed toward an understanding that you need time alone.

During the last twenty-five years at Concord Church, I did not attend any social events on Saturdays except funerals and weddings, though a funeral might not be seen as a social event. Because there was always something going on every Saturday, I suppose that there were complaints from time to time. I said to the people one way or the other, both casually and directly, that if they expected me to bring a helpful message on Sunday, I needed to have time. I think that people respect that. Now, of course, the people need to see some evidence on Sunday that something good resulted from the time they have allotted the preacher!

TAKING CARE OF THE FAMILY

Avery Lee: When the pastor takes the family for a vacation, it should be a true vacation, not a so-called working vacation. Don't be tempted to work on sermons. Make a point of having fun.

As a minister of the gospel, the tendency is to put one's work first. This is totally understandable. The truth is, however, that sometimes it's the pastor's ego that may be operating—the feeling that nothing good can happen without you. The older I got as a Christian, the more I believed in the priority of the family. I do not regret having put my family first on many occasions. I see the necessity of more people giving more time and attention to their own families. The home is fast losing its place as the basic unit of society. The home needs a Christian reinstatement of priority.

Too many pastors have neglected their families, and this is to their detriment. Yes, the women's fellowship or that cantankerous deacon needs soothing attention. So does your family. When it comes to time spent with family, a lot is said about "quality time" versus "quantity time." I suspect that quality time is invoked sometimes to assuage a sense of guilt over too little quantity time.

Even in the midst of all of the church's demands, I urge pastors to take time to see your daughter or son in the school drama. Go ahead and miss a prayer meeting to see your daughter play in the district basketball playoff. Drive three hundred miles to hear your son play in the symphony orchestra. It's worth it in the long run.

On one occasion I flew from New Orleans to Knoxville to see my son run in a track meet. While I was sitting in the athletic dining hall at the University of Tennessee, a brawny football player came up to me and said wistfully, "Dr. Lee, it's good to have you here. You know, my dad has never seen me play ball." His words stung me.

Take care of your own family. To lose your family is almost as bad as losing your soul. Song of Solomon 1:6 states, "They made me keeper of the vineyards, but my own vineyard I did not keep." Never let it be said of the pastor, "But my own vineyard I did not keep."

Gardner Taylor: You cannot go out to save the world and let your own family be lost. In fact, pastors will find that the better they are able to deal with the people at home, the better they will be able to deal with people outside the home. Pastors and their spouses and children need to continue doing the things that they have always enjoyed doing. Both of my wives liked the theater, and so we went often. In addition to enjoying it, I got a lot of good preaching ideas.

TIME FOR SELF

Avery Lee: The people in my congregation understood that morning time was my time. People knew that if my door was closed, they should leave me alone. And I spent a lot of that time reading. Some of it was religious literature, but a lot of it was just for fun. Even in my eighties I still read at least one work of fiction every week. People need to give the pastor the freedom to enjoy life.

Gardner Taylor: I advise pastors to exercise as often as possible. For many years I worked out regularly at the Harlem YMCA. Physical activity is good for the body and is also good for the mind.

I started playing golf in 1953 or thereabout, and that helped a great deal. My mother, who lived with us in Brooklyn for the last eight years of her life, would see me practicing my swing in the driveway and would say, "It looks like it takes your mind off everything." She was right. Pastors need some diversion. They need to find some activity that is ultimately not important, but at the moment consumes you altogether.

SPIRITUAL FORMATION

Gardner Taylor: Pastors, like others, ought to carve out time in their schedules for personal devotions. I do not sleep well early at night, so nights have been my best time for reflection. But there is a freshness about the morning that makes it ideal for many. The time of day is not important. What's important is setting aside some time every day. I practiced, not always successfully, what Alexander Maclaren called "sitting silent before God." It's not praying. It's not reading. It's just opening yourself to whatever God wishes to say. It is amazing what can happen.

Young ministers have to be available for what the Lord is saying to them. Making oneself available to God can be difficult and sometimes painful. One way to hide from the pain of facing up to God is through a lot of activity—keeping busy. We can hide from God in a lot of ways. Even reading the Scripture can be a way to avoid this encounter. You must be willing to look deep within yourself before God. It can be a painful encounter as we ask, "What are my strengths and my weaknesses? What are the things that I dare not mention to any human being? That I almost dare not mention to myself? How, by God's grace, can that element in my personality be dealt with?"

One of the tragedies of our generation is its fear of silence. We see all these people walking around with cell phones seemingly glued to their heads. I think that people are afraid to be alone. But you cannot come to a sense of who you are and who you ought to be, and of where you are and where you ought to be, without silent times and personal pondering before God.

Our culture, including the church culture, places too much emphasis on doing instead of on being. Many pastors have been bitten by this bug. They feel that they have to be always doing something in order to justify themselves to a society that does not value the work of the pastor as much as it once did.

SOME CLOSING WORDS

"THE BEST ADVICE I EVER RECEIVED"

Gardner Taylor: My mother, after having been a pastor's wife for some thirty years, said to me, "Gardner, you must not be so far from people that they cannot get to you, but you must not be a doormat, or they will walk over you." This is good advice for everyone, but especially for pastors. It's important to find the right balance between respecting other people and making sure that they respect you.

Avery Lee: Most of us are familiar with this line from Shakespeare's play *Hamlet*: "To thine own self be true, and it must follow, as the night the day, thou canst not then be false to any man." Unless we can be true to ourselves first, we cannot be true to others.

ON BEING A PASTOR IN THE TWENTY-FIRST CENTURY

Gardner Taylor: I feel enormous compassion for younger people entering the ministry today, because they are being pulled in so many different directions and must contend with so many more distractions. I recall as a child living next door to Miss Anna Mathews. She had a radio; it was the only radio in the neighborhood. These days, in some households there's a television in every room. We are bombarded from every side by advertisements or the latest technological craze. It's harder and harder to find a time for stillness.

Also, the political polarization of our society has been well documented. Everyone is angry and on the attack, snarling at each other. Cable television has contributed to the dumbing down of our political discourse; it has made it more violent. Rational discourse has all but disappeared. I don't think that we can go on with this polarization. Everything has a hard edge to it. One of the jobs of the preacher of today and tomorrow is to soften this hard edge.

ON BEING AN ASSOCIATE PASTOR

Avery Lee: Pastors should not be in a hurry to become the head leader of a church. Filling the role of an associate pastor is a perfect opportunity to learn under a mentor. As an associate pastor, the buck does not stop with you, but you are privy to all that goes on.

Being a part of church staff meetings without feeling the pressure of having to solve all the church's problems is a good place for a young person to be. You can learn in two years as an associate what it would take at least twice that amount of time to learn on your own.

One of the best things I learned as an associate was the truth of the Boy Scout motto, "Be prepared." One Sunday, just before the service, the head pastor called in sick and I had to enter the pulpit with no prepared sermon. From then on, I always had at least one sermon in the pocket. This was just one of many ways being an associate helped an embryonic pastor learn the ropes.

SOME "DO'S AND DON'TS" FOR MALE PASTORS

Avery Lee: Don't ever refer to your spouse as "the little woman." Don't ever, for heaven's sake and yours, forget her birthday or your anniversary. Don't ever take her for granted. Do love her. Love her! Love her! Keep the fires of romance burning. Listen to her; her intuitive insights are valuable. Surprise her with flowers at times other than special occasions. Take home a rose when you leave the office. Take time to be alone, if only for one night in a motel. Get a sitter or farm out the kids. Do your share of cooking and other household chores, including laundry.

ON MALE PASTORS AVOIDING TEMPTATION

Avery Lee: Obviously, a male pastor's life entails ministering to women. There are women of whom I've been fond, maybe even felt a kind of love for. My second wife, Glad, once said that I had a harem of such women. These women were dear friends. Can a man and a woman have a platonic love? Certainly. But there's always "the temptation of possibility." And that spells T-R-O-U-B-L-E!

I can speak, of course, only from the vantage point of a male pastor. I believe that it's important for the pastor to know himself and his limitations. Some pastors will never visit with a woman unless he's accompanied by his wife or some other person. I don't advise making this an absolute rule. After all, you can't prevent all the gossip, no matter how hard you try to avoid it.

Keep in mind this insight that has been variously attributed to George Bernard Shaw, Tennyson, and Oscar Wilde: "Men always want to be a woman's first love. Women have a more subtle instinct: what they like is to be a man's last romance." Be your wife's last romance, and she yours. Remember, both of you said, "Till death do us part."

ON THE CURRENT STATE OF PREACHING

Gardner Taylor: I am profoundly concerned about what people, particularly in black churches, but in all churches, are hearing from television preachers, so many of whom have virtually reduced the gospel to a budgetary matter with their quid pro quo, "name it and claim it" theology. This commercialization is injurious to the gospel and can be disillusioning for believers.

Cable television has harmed the faith and the whole society in part by contributing to preaching that lacks intellectual depth. I'm not talking about intellectual snobbery. My father in the 1920s was not highly educated, but his preaching addressed the issues of the day with a kind of substance that's largely absent from the church today. Much of what I witness today is a "cross-less" Christianity, a happiness cult. It's heresy, but it's appealing. And for a few moments, it will win the day. But it's not real, and I don't believe that it can go on.

I'm also disturbed by some of the antics I see being displayed in the pulpit. Much preaching has come to be characterized by emotion without substance. Emotion is important, but it ought to rise out of a proclamation of substantive truth and shared experience.

ON KNOWING WHEN IT'S TIME TO GO

Avery Lee: There comes that time when a pastor faces the question "Is it time to move on?" One day at lunch my current pastor asked, "Avery, when do you know that it's time to change pastorates?" I replied, "I don't know. Something deep inside will say, 'This is the right time.'" To that I would add that it's best to change when things are going right rather than when things are going wrong.

Twice, the pastoral search committee of the St. Charles Avenue Baptist Church in New Orleans had asked me to be their pastor. I had preached there in the 1940s and again in the 1950s. Even though this was the only church I ever coveted, I declined both times. The timing wasn't right. There were still battles in Ruston, with the integration of the public schools being the major one. In 1961—a gap of eight years since the first invitation—another committee came back to ask me again. The third time was the charm. It was time.

ON ATTENDING YOUR FORMER CHURCH

Avery Lee: Pastors who reside in the area of their former church must decide whether to attend upon retiring. My general advice is, "If you feel comfortable, stay." The pastor must make this determination along with his or her family. It's important, however, to consider the possible effects on the church. Some new pastors feel threatened if a former pastor stays around, while others will view a retired pastor as a mentor. The retired pastor ought to honor the new pastor's wishes.

If you do stay, I recommend taking an extended vacation, maybe even an interim pastorate. And I strongly advise against keeping an office in the church. Also, do not listen to complaints about the new pastor. Those who are complaining probably said the same things about you.

In my case, I returned to New Orleans and rejoined my old church after a five-year absence during which I served another church. I resolved to be as inconspicuous as possible. I believe that the retired pastor should refuse to serve on any committees, should refuse to offer opinions, and should offer advice only when asked. A retired pastor should preach when asked by the present pastor. And certainly, don't tell the new pastor about the "problem people" in the church. The new pastor might have a different set.

Communication is important. The pastor who preceded me said, "Avery, if my remaining in the church as a member will cause you any problems, I'll join another church." I told him that I wasn't sure I wanted to be at the church if he didn't stay. He had resigned to become a chaplain and director of Clinical Pastoral Education at a local Baptist hospital. He became my best referral for those who needed counseling.

THE NEED FOR A PROPHETIC WORD

Gardner Taylor: These may be the musings of old age, but I don't see our society being able to continue down the current path for very long. We are suffering from the disease of materialism. Soon, I believe, our society will be sated and will be almost vomiting in revolt and in search of something much more real than material things.

For this and for other reasons, this is a great day for a prophetic word. It may not be a popular word, but when a nation reaches the pinnacle of power, it's in an awfully perilous position. I wonder if preachers, white and black, are able to speak prophetically to society. But we need preachers who will try. Prophetic preaching is not angry preaching; it's not "attack dog" preaching. It needs to come up out of Scripture. And it must begin with the preacher's recognition that he or she is a part of the disease that's being preached about.

We must oppose materialism at every turn. I don't think that we realize how critical this is for a society in which things have become gods. Scherer had a great line to summarize this when he described the Sunday worship service as a time when we ought to bring the gods that we have made before the God who made us.

ON GROWING OLD

Avery Lee: William Herbert Carruth wrote in the poem "Ghosts of Dreams" that "there's not much to do, but to bury a man when the last of his dreams is dead." That's what I believe. After seeing the musical *Man of La Mancha*, I wrote a sermon based on the song "The Impossible Dream," and I consider it my signature sermon. For me, having come from humble roots, being able to go to a university and then on to one of the nation's top seminaries was an all-but-impossible dream. I have always been a dreamer of dreams, and I hope I always will be.

After more than sixty years as a minister of the gospel, I, along with Robert Browning, can say, "Grow old along with me; the best is yet to be." Yes, there were some things that ought not to have been done, and some needed things that were left undone. And there will be those things for you too. But we do the best we can in our circumstances as we face the constant challenge of trying to bring the *Is* and the *Ought* closer together.

Some people walk with a backward glance, wistfully yearning for "the good old days." I prefer to walk toward the dawn, not the sunset, looking forward, not backward. I recall a country song that refers to walking out of a room backward so that they'll think you're coming in. I can look back with thanks for yesterday, even as I look forward to tomorrow. Or as Dag Hammarskjöld put it, "For all that has been, thanks. For all that will be, yes."

NOTES

The Pastor's Role and Work

1. Leslie Weatherhead, *This Is the Victory* (New York and Nashville: Abingdon-Cokesbury Press, 1941), 165.

2. For a delightful look at Jewish humor, see *The Big Book of Jewish Humor*, ed. William Novak and Moshe Waldoks (New York: Harper & Row, 1981).— Ed.

3. Theodor Reik, *Listening with the Third Ear: The Inner Experience of a Psychoanalyst* (New York: Farrar, Straus, 1948).

Study

1. A new version of this twelve-volume set is now in print: *The New Interpreter's Bible*, ed. Leander E. Keck (12 vols.; Nashville: Abingdon Press, 1994–1999).—Ed.

ABOUT THE AUTHORS

AVERY LEE

A native of Oklahoma City, G. Avery Lee was born on March 3, 1916. His mother passed away when he was only three, and his father moved away, leaving Avery to be reared by his grandmother. An avid reader since childhood, he aspired to go to college. Someone in the church offered to pay tuition at Hardin-Simmons University in Abilene, Texas, from which Avery graduated in 1939.

He'd dreamed of going to seminary at Yale but didn't think he could get accepted. A high school teacher persuaded him that it would cost a mere three-cent stamp to find out. He was accepted, but this was the Depression era, and the young man had no money. The same teacher persuaded young Avery to invest another three-cent stamp to inquire about a scholarship. It was a good investment.

Dr. Lee graduated from Yale Divinity School in 1944. After graduating, he accepted a position as associate pastor at First Baptist Church in Baton Rouge, Louisiana. Following that he served as pastor at University Baptist Church in Champagne, Illinois, and then at First Baptist of Ruston, Louisiana. But it was at St. Charles Avenue Baptist Church in New Orleans, which he served from 1961 to 1980, where he would make his greatest mark.

Throughout his ministry, Dr. Lee was known for his sharp wit, his substantive and provocative sermons, and his willingness to take a stand on social issues, especially in the area of race relations. Says current St. Charles Avenue pastor Steven Meriwether, "People who were here in the '60s and '70s remember Avery Lee as the best pastor this church has ever had. During that time, his was a voice like none other."

In the 1980s, Dr. Lee came out of retirement to serve for five years as pastor at University Baptist Church in Hattiesburg, Mississippi. He returned to New Orleans to serve two stints as interim pastor at St. Charles before retiring for good. Dr. Lee's first marriage ended after 30 years in 1972 with the death of his wife, Ann, whom he'd met while at Hardin-Simmons. He remarried in 1974. His second wife, Gladys "Glad" Lee, passed away in 2002. In 1998, the Avery and Glad Lee Preaching Series was inaugurated in honor of Dr. and Mrs. Lee.

GARDNER CALVIN TAYLOR

Gardner Calvin Taylor, a living legend once dubbed by *Time* magazine as the nation's "Dean of African American Preaching," was born on June 18, 1918, in Baton Rouge, Louisiana. As a college student at Leland College, a black

Baptist college located in nearby Baker, Louisiana, he excelled in various extracurricular activities, especially debate.

In 1937, he enrolled at Oberlin (Ohio) Graduate School of Theology, from which he graduated in 1940. This was the same year he married Laura Scott, with whom he shared over five decades of marriage before her passing in February of 1995.

While still at Oberlin, Dr. Taylor took on his first pastorate, at Bethany Baptist Church in Elyria, Ohio. Upon graduating, he became pastor at Beulah Baptist Church in New Orleans. In 1943, he became pastor at his home church, Mt. Zion Baptist, in Baton Rouge.

Five years later, at the age of thirty, he became pastor at Concord Baptist Church in Brooklyn, New York, a ministry that would span forty-two years, until his retirement in 1990. During Dr. Taylor's tenure at Concord, the church grew from six thousand members to over fifteen thousand.

Beginning in 1959, Dr. Taylor delivered messages for the National Radio Vespers Hour. This program had been created by the National Broadcasting Company so that the preaching of Harry Emerson Fosdick could be heard nationwide.

Through the years, Dr. Taylor's mastery of the art of preaching, rooted in thorough biblical scholarship, earned him the distinction among many as the world's greatest living African American preacher. In 2000, Dr. Taylor received the Presidential Medal of Freedom, the nation's highest civilian award.

Dr. Taylor remarried in July of 1996. He and his wife, Phillis, now reside in Raleigh, North Carolina.

BOOKS BY THE AUTHORS

BOOKS BY G. AVERY LEE

Life's Everyday Questions (1953)
Preaching from Ecclesiastes (1958)
What's Right with the Church? (1967)
Great Men of the Bible and the Women in Their Lives (1968)
The Roads to God (1969)
The Reputation of a Church (1970)
Where Christian Ideas Take Shape in People: The Unfolding
   Drama of a Church (1973)
I Want That Mountain! (1974)
The Glorious Company (1986)
Elijah: Yahweh Is My God (1987)
Affirmations of a Skeptical Believer (1991)
Living in the Meantime (1994)
The Bible: Read It Again for the First Time (1995)
Take Me Home, Country Road (1998)
Our Name Is Baptist: 100 Years of Faith in Action: St. Charles
   Avenue Baptist Church, 1898–1998 (1998)

BOOKS BY GARDNER C. TAYLOR

How Shall They Preach? (1977)
Chariots Aflame (1988)
The Scarlet Thread (1981)
We Have This Ministry (1996, with Samuel D. Proctor)

The Words of Gardner Taylor
(available both in hardcover and paperback)
Volume 1: NBC Radio Sermons, 1959–1970
Volume 2: Sermons from the Middle Years, 1970–1980
Volume 3: Quintessential Classics, 1980–Present
Volume 4: Special Occasion and Expository Sermons
Volume 5: Lectures, Essays, and Interviews
Volume 6: 50 Years of Timeless Treasures

Audio Resources:
Essential Taylor (two compact disks or audiocassettes)
Essential Taylor II (two compact disks or audiocassettes)

SPEAKERS AT THE AVERY AND GLAD LEE PREACHING SERIES

Gardner C. Taylor (inaugural speaker, 1998)
Paul D. Duke (1999)
Martin Marty (2000)
Barbara Brown Taylor (2001)
Bill J. Leonard (2002)
Jean Bethke Elshtain (2002)
Fisher Humphreys (2003)
Roger Olson (2004)